Máquinas maravillosas/Mighty Machines

Tractores agrícolas/ Farm Tractors

por/by Matt Doeden

Traducción/Translation: Dr. Martín Luis Guzmán Ferrer

Editor Consultor/Consulting Editor: Dra. Gail Saunders-Smith

Consultor/Consultant: Kristin Harner
Public Relations/Foundation Director
Minnesota Farm Bureau

Capstone

Mankato, Minnesota

Pebble Plus is published by Capstone Press,
151 Good Counsel Drive, P.O. Box 669, Mankato, Minnesota 56002.
www.capstonepress.com

1 2 3 4 5 6 13 12 11 10 09 08

Library of Congress Cataloging-in-Publication Data
Doeden, Matt.
    [Farm tractors. Spanish & English]
    Tractores agrícolas / por Matt Doeden = Farm tractors / by Matt Doeden.
    p. cm. — (Pebble Plus. Máquinas maravillosas = Pebble Plus. Mighty machines)
    ISBN-13: 978-1-4296-2375-9 (hardcover)
    ISBN-10: 1-4296-2375-6 (hardcover)
    1. Farm tractors — Juvenile literature. I. Title.
S711.D58518 2009
631.3'72 — dc22   2008001255

Summary: Simple text and photographs describe farm tractors, their parts, and what they do — in both English
    and Spanish.

Editorial Credits
Mari Schuh, editor; Katy Kudela, bilingual editor; Eida del Risco, Spanish copy editor; Molly Nei, set designer;
    Patrick D. Dentinger, book designer; Jo Miller, photo researcher/photo editor

Photo Credits
Bruce Coleman Inc./Michael Black, 5
Capstone Press/Karon Dubke, cover, 1, 8–9, 10–11
Corbis/Ed Bock, 21
OneBlueShoe, 6–7, 13
Richard Hamilton Smith, 14–15
Shutterstock/Peter Baxter, 16–17
SuperStock/Buck Miller, 19

Note to Parents and Teachers

The Máquinas maravillosas/Mighty Machines set supports national social studies standards
related to science, technology, and society. This book describes and illustrates farm tractors
in both English and Spanish. The images support early readers in understanding the text.
The repetition of words and phrases helps early readers learn new words. This book also
introduces early readers to subject-specific vocabulary words, which are defined in the
Glossary section. Early readers may need assistance to read some words and to use the
Table of Contents, Glossary, Internet Sites, and Index sections of the book.

Table of Contents

Tabla de contenidos

Farm Tractors

Tractors are pulling machines.
Farmers use tractors to pull
other farm machines.

Tractores agrícolas

Los tractores son máquinas
para jalar. Los granjeros
usan los tractores para jalar
otras máquinas agrícolas.

Tractor Parts

Tractors have big bumpy tires. The bumps help tractors move across fields.

Las partes de los tractores

Los tractores tienen unas ruedas con relieves. Los relieves sirven para que los tractores se muevan a través de los campos.

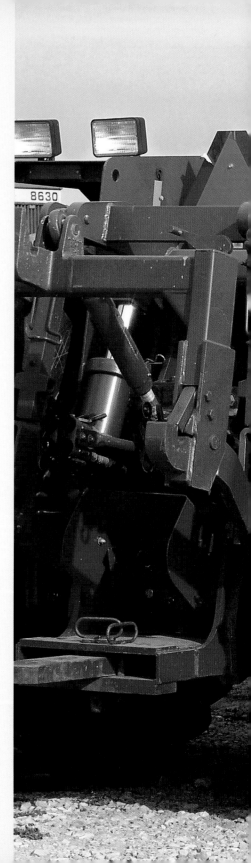

Farmers sit inside
the cab to drive
the tractor.

Los granjeros se sientan
en la cabina del tractor
para manejarlo.

Farmers use a
steering wheel to
turn the tractor.

Los granjeros usan
el volante para hacer
girar el tractor.

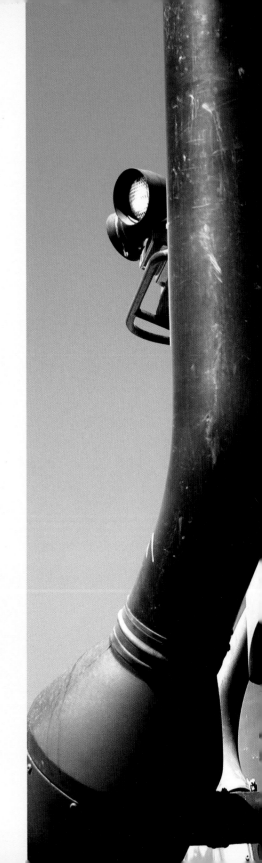

Tractors have hitches.

Machines hook
onto hitches.

Los tractores tienen enganches.

Las máquinas se sujetan
en esos enganches.

Pulling Power

Tractors pull planters
that drop seeds
in the field.

Fuerza para jalar

Los tractores jalan
las sembradoras que
arrojan las semillas en
los campos de cultivo.

Tractors pull sprayers

to kill weeds.

Los tractores jalan las bombas

para fumigar que matan

las malas hierbas.

Tractors pull balers
that roll hay.

Los tractores jalan
las embaladoras que
enrollan la paja.

Mighty Machines

Tractors help farmers
grow crops. Tractors
are mighty machines.

Máquinas maravillosas

Los tractores ayudan a
los granjeros a cultivar
sus cosechas. Los tractores
son máquinas maravillosas.

Glossary

baler — a machine that rolls or presses hay into round or square bales

cab — the part of a tractor where a farmer sits

crop — a plant farmers grow in large amounts, usually for food; farmers grow crops such as corn, soybeans, and peas.

hitch — the part of a tractor that other machines hook onto

planter — a machine that drops seeds evenly into rows

sprayer — a machine that sprays and kills weeds

Glosario

la bomba para fumigar — máquina que fumiga y mata las malas hierbas

la cabina — parte del tractor donde se sienta el granjero

la cosecha — planta que el granjero cultiva en grandes cantidades; los granjeros cosechan maíz, trigo y chícharos.

la embaladora — máquina que enrolla o prensa la paja en bultos redondos o cuadrados

el enganche — parte del tractor donde se sujetan otras máquinas

la sembradora — máquina que arroja semillas en los surcos ordenadamente

Internet Sites

FactHound offers a safe, fun way to find Internet sites related to this book. All of the sites on FactHound have been researched by our staff.

Here's how:

1. Visit *www.facthound.com*

2. Choose your grade level.

3. Type in this book ID **1429623756** for age-appropriate sites. You may also browse subjects by clicking on letters, or by clicking on pictures and words.

4. Click on the **Fetch It** button.

FactHound will fetch the best sites for you!

Index

Sitios de Internet

FactHound te brinda una manera divertida y segura de encontrar sitios de Internet relacionados con este libro. Hemos investigado todos los sitios de FactHound. Es posible que algunos sitios no estén en español.

Se hace así:

1. Visita *www.facthound.com*

2. Elige tu grado escolar.

3. Introduce este código especial **1429623756** para ver sitios apropiados a tu edad, o usa una palabra relacionada con este libro para hacer una búsqueda general.

4. Haz un clic en el botón **Fetch It**.

¡FactHound buscará los mejores sitios para ti!

Índice